You Can't Take Away What You Give Away

The Poems of Itka Frajman Zygmuntowicz

by Itka Frajman Zygmuntowicz Copyright 1996

© Itka Frajman Zygmuntowicz, 2008

All rights reserved. Unauthorized reproduction of this book or its contents by xerography, facsimile, or other means is illegal, except for brief quotations in reviews or articles.

ISBN – 13: 978-1449539832
ISBN – 10: 1449539831

Cover Layout by
Lourdes Jaramillo

Book Layout by
Debbie Zygmuntowicz

Dedication

To the sacred Memory of all
those voices that have been
silenced forever in the Holocaust
from 1933 - 1945

TABLE OF CONTENTS

The Seed of Love 1

No Graves, No Headstones, No Markers 2

Where Are You, My Brothers? 4

Show Your Face 6

My Grandma 7

America, My Country 8

The Bridge of Love: Dialogue 9

A Nazi Murderer in Snow White Gloves 10

A World That Vanished 12

The Silent Voice 14

I Know You 17

My Love Belongs to All 18

Life's Dream 19

Just 20

Clipped Wings 21

Sing Little Bird 22

Sing 23

Spring 24

In My Soul I See Thee 25

The Spark of Hate 26

You Can Be My Friend 27

I Can't Be You	28
Do Not Forget Us	29
I Am Not a Number	31
For Everything There Is a Season	33
The Most Valuable Gift	34
One Day I Shall Die	35
Who Wrote On Your Arm?	36
Puzzles	38
I Don't Want To Be Like Cain or Abel	39
I Know	40
Little Things	41
Words and Deeds	42
The Power of Words	43
The Secret of Finding Peace of Mind	44

The Seed of Love

With God all things are possible,
Regardless how remote they are.
The seed of love is the strongest seed,
The strongest seed by far.

Rooted deep in the heart of man,
It nourishes and feeds the soul.
The seed of love is the strongest seed,
The strongest seed of all.

It helps to heal and to endure,
To create, to share and give.
The seed of love is the strongest seed,
For it gives you the will to live.

by Itka Frajman Zygmuntowicz May 26, 1978
Copyright 1995

No Graves, No Headstones, No Markers

No graves, no headstones, no markers,
You have vanished in agony, smoke, and flames.
Bereft and broken hearted,
On my soul are engraved your names.

I can't forget you, dear sisters and brothers,
I remember your anguish and cry.
Six million innocent Jewish men, women, and little children,
They did not want to die!

They fought so valiantly and courageously,
As partisans in the Second World War.
They fought in the Warsaw Ghetto uprising,
When they realized what Hitler had for them in store.

They fought in the Vilna Ghetto Underground,
In the ghettos of Kovna, Byalistock, Minsk and others.

They fought with courage and heroism,
To defend the honor of their sisters and brothers.

They fought in the Nazi killing centers,
Struggling so hard to stay alive.
They fought under diabolical conditions,
Morally and spiritually to survive.

They fought the defiling of God's name,
While the world stood so silently by.
Six million innocent Jewish men, women and little children,
O God! They did not want to die!

by Itka Frajman Zygmuntowicz   February 12, 1980
Copyright 1995

Where Are You, My Brothers?

Where are you, my brothers, where are you all?
I still see your faces and hear you call.
I have not forgotten you, dear mother and father,
Or you, my little sister Zysl, and Srulek, my brother.

I have not forgotten the love that we shared,
Your loyalty and devotion and the way you had cared.
I have not forgotten my aunts, uncles, cousins, and friends,
They all died so young by the bloody Nazi hands.

With the exception of just a few, the world stood by so still,
And millions of innocent Jewish people permitted to kill.
Auschwitz, Treblinka, Buchenwald, Maidanek and so many more.
Who could imagine what Hitler had for us in store?

Who could believe that doctors and
nurses were trained to kill?
And engineers to build gas chambers with
such great skill?
Who could think that to be born a Jew
was a crime,
And that God's chosen people would be
scapegoats all the time.

It's ironic that the so called "Superior
Aryan" race,
Could commit mass murder and disgrace
the human face.
How presumptuous of man to take what
he didn't give,
And make a decision who shall die and
who shall live.

by Itka Frajman Zygmuntowicz   December 7, 1977
Copyright 1996

Show Your Face

Show your face, at least in a dream.
I wake up in terror and hear your scream.
Your images I see in ashes and flames,
Yet still I can hear you calling my name.
Show your face, I am so alone.
My mother and father and brothers are gone.
They left me behind to carry the pain,
And to see that their death shall not be in vain.
Show your face so my children can see,
The roots of our chopped off family tree.
Heal the branches with your faith and love,
Until we are united in heaven above.

by Itka Frajman Zygmuntowicz   1978
Copyright 1996

My Grandma

My Grandma was old,
My Grandma was wise,
She gave me so much love,
She gave me good advice.

My dear sweet old Grandma
So often used to say,
"My child, you only have
What you give away."

So don't spare a hug,
A kiss or a smile.
Remember, dear child,
We are here just for a while.

I loved my sweet old Grandma
But suddenly one day,
My dear sweet old Grandma
Forever went away.

But her love and words of wisdom,
Are with me till this day,
"My child, you only have
What you give away."

by Itka Frajman Zygmuntowicz   November 25, 1989
Copyright 1996

America, My Country

America, my country,
You are a great land,
To the homeless and oppressed,
You extend a helping hand.

I found here freedom,
To work, pray, and play,
And so many new opportunities,
To learn and grow each day.

America, my country,
I'm so grateful to be here,
Where I no longer have to live,
In constant terror and fear.

Where the gas chambers of Auschwitz
Are far, far behind,
Where I have the right,
To freely speak my mind.

America, my country,
I love you so dearly,
And for all my blessings,
I thank God and you sincerely.

by Itka Frajman Zygmuntowicz   November 22, 1979
Copyright 1996

The Bridge of Love: Dialogue

"Hello! Who are you?"
"I am a human being;
I am God's child
And my parents' child."
 "And so am I."

"I am a member of the human family.
I love my family,
And what I love I work for."
 "And so do I."

"I came from my mother's womb
To enjoy Father Time for a while.
And when my time on earth is up,
I shall return to the womb of the earth."
 "And so will I."

 "But in the meantime, let us build
Bridges of communication
Instead of walls of isolation.
It will surely please God above when all his children
Will meet on the bridge of love."

 by Itka Frajman Zygmuntowicz July 11, 1983
Copyright 1996

A Nazi Murderer in Snow White Gloves

Snow white gloves are shrouding his blood-stained hands,
And his soul is as black as the night of the Holocaust.
I remember him well standing at the gate of the killing center of Auschwitz
In his spotless SS uniform and a swastika on his armband.
He looks so calm, collected, and so convincingly deceptive,
Intoxicated by the myth of his racial purity and innate superiority.
He willfully carries out Hitler's evil will, instead of God's divine will.
In his right gloved hand, he holds a truncheon and points it,
Sometimes to the right and sometimes to the left,
Selecting who shall live and who shall die.
He is a Nazi murderer in snow white gloves,
A university educated man with two doctoral degrees.
He is the infamous Dr. Josef Mengele, Birkenau's Angel of Death.

He knows how to heal the sick,
But perversely chooses to kill healthy Jews
Enslaved in the Killing Center of Auschwitz.
More than 400,000 innocent men, women, and little children died at his hands,
And among them my entire family of blessed memory
Was murdered on November 22, 1942, in the gas chambers of Auschwitz.

by Itka Frajman Zygmuntowicz
Survivor of the Killing Center of Auschwitz   April 29, 1982
Copyright 1996

A World That Vanished

Just like a leaf tossed to the wind
Separated from its branches and tree,
Not belonging anymore
Liberated but not free;
Carrying the pain of separation
Memories so painful and dear,
Memories of a world that used to be
A world that is no longer here.

I still see the Sabbath candles
And my Mother's gentle face,
My Father is chanting the prayers
My Grandmother with her white shawl of lace;
I see my little sister and brother
So young and so full of cheer,
Not yet understanding prejudice and
hatred but sensing uncertainty and fear.

The Nazi boots are marching
My world with terror is filled,
The holy scriptures are burning
Children are starved, tortured, and killed;
The Ghettos are closing us in
What is there for us in store?
My world is growing smaller and smaller,
Nothing is like it was before.

The freight trains are taking us on a journey
For most it is their last ride,
My sister and brother are burning
There is no more place to hide;
Hitler's final solution is sealed
We are trapped in a world of hell.
I am amazed that I have survived,
The story of the Holocaust to tell.

by Itka Frajman Zygmuntowicz   May 18, 1978
Copyright 1996

The Silent Voice

Dedicated to all those whose voices have been silenced forever in the Holocaust from 1933-1945

When ages of civilization crumble to dust,
And death is raging supreme,
When the devil is crowned by the power of deceit,
Then freedom is a faraway dream.

When all that you loved is taken from you,
And you are stripped to the bare bone,
When all moral boundaries and laws are broken,
Then you are in hell with Satan alone!

When Jews are depicted as subhuman, as "vermin,"
And brute force and evil prevail,
When doctors and nurses turn children to corpses,
Then all logic and reason fail!

When the whole world remains dead silent,
With the exception of just a few,
Then they grant Satan license and opportunity,
To murder in the gas chambers a God-loving Jew!

When men and women are kept apart,
And new life is not conceived,
When there is no sound of laughter or song,
How can God by man be perceived?

When mass murder of the Jews becomes legal,
Under the banner of an ideology or God's sacred name,
Then it is not the victims, but the Nazi murderers,
Who did not resist Satan and defiled God's name.

When living skeletons are marching at gun point,
Through the gate of Auschwitz in long columns of five,
Cold, starved, forced to hard labor,
What power on earth gave them the strength to survive?

When all heads are shaved, all human rights denied,
And all wear the same kind of tattered striped dress,
When the worship of God becomes a crime,
Then the whole world is in a very terrible mess!

When Hitler's dream becomes a reality,
And the Nazis send Jews to the left and to the right,
Then such men are not ruled by God's divine power,
But by their own burning ambition for power and might.

When the so called "Superior Aryan" Nazi race,
Used all their knowledge, technology, and skill,
To murder six million Jews merely for being born Jewish,
That was not God's, but Hitler's demonic will!

by Itka Frajman Zygmuntowicz   May 11, 1980
Copyright 1996

I Know You

I know you by the way
 You treat me,
And by the way
 You make me feel inside.
Those things tell me
 A lot about you,
Those things, my friend,
 You cannot hide.
It's not your color,
 Your religion, or occupation
That tell me
 Who you are;
It's your deeds
 Of kindness or of cruelty,
That tell me
 Much more by far.

by Itka Frajman Zygmuntowicz   May 11, 1978
Copyright 1996

My Love Belongs to All

My body belongs to me,
To God belongs my soul,
To my children belongs my inheritance,
My love belongs to all.

by Itka Frajman Zygmuntowicz   February 3, 1978
Copyright 1996

Life's Dream

So many mountains, so many streams,
So many hopes, such endless dreams.
I yearn to fill my empty cup
And drink life's joy and never stop.

To sing, to dance, not be afraid,
To open every door and gate,
To the fullest I'd like to live,
I'd like to love, to share, and give.

And taste of every fruit and vine,
With kings and beggars I'd like to dine,
And be prepared the day my ship
Will sail me out on a heavenly trip.

by Itka Frajman Zygmuntowicz   June 11, 1967
Copyright 1996

Just

Just a woman simple and plain
Just a wife without worldly fame
Just a mother with hopes and fears
Just a friend to share laughter or tears
Just a neighbor with a helping hand
Just a citizen of a mighty land
Just a child of a heavenly Father
With the right to live like any other.

by Itka Frajman Zygmuntowicz   August 24, 1966
Copyright 1996

Clipped Wings

I feel like a bird
With clipped wings,
Tied to the earth
By invisible strings.

Chained to a destiny
I did not choose,
I feel like a prisoner
Who cannot break loose.

I look at the sky
With a heavy sigh,
But my wings have been clipped
And I cannot fly.

by Itka Frajman Zygmuntowicz   February 14, 1967
Copyright 1996

Sing Little Bird

Sing, little bird,
Sing me a song,
Heal my sorrow and pain.
Sing, my little bird,
Don't ever stop,
Your song is not in vain.

Sing, little bird,
Sing me a song,
Don't worry that no one is near.
Sing, my little bird,
For so long as you sing,
The voice of God I can hear.

by Itka Frajman Zygmuntowicz   May 30, 1980
Copyright 1996

Sing

Sing, sing, leave behind your sorrow,
Sing, sing, fill your heart with joy.
Sing, sing, fill the world with laughter,
Sing and don't worry about tomorrow.
Just keep on singing,
And have a good time.

Just keep on singing,
And have a good time.

by Itka Frajmar Zygmuntowicz   May 30, 1980
Copyright 1996

Spring

The grass is green,
The leaves are dancing.
There's a song in my heart,
I feel like romancing.

The flowers are in blossom,
So red, white, and pink.
The sun is golden yellow.
It's spring, it's spring!

My soul has wings
And wants to fly,
Just like a little bluebird
High in the sky.

My soul has wings.

My soul has wings.

by Itka Frajman Zygmuntowicz   May 27, 1980
Copyright 1996

In My Soul I See Thee

In the ripples of the ocean,
In the depth of the sea,
In the eyes of a child,
In my soul I see Thee.

In the flowers and in the tree,
In the richness of the land,
In the grandeur of the universe,
I see the handwriting of thy hand.

In the sun and the stars,
In the butterfly and in the bee,
In all of your holy creation,
In my soul I see Thee.

by Itka Frajman Zygmuntowicz   April 29, 1980
Copyright 1996

The Spark of Hate

When we open
The door to hate,
We are closing the door
To the heavenly gate.

Hate like a monster
Lurks in the dark,
And just like fire
Begins with a spark.

Hate destroys
Our peace of mind
And is always
A threat to all humankind.

by Itka Frajman Zygmuntowicz   December 18, 1977
Copyright 1996

You Can Be My Friend

You can be my friend,
But not if you keep on hurting me.
You cannot have it both ways,
Don't you see?

I will not voluntarily
Accept or inflict pain on others.
For we are all God's children,
We are all sisters and brothers.

If you need my help,
I will gladly lend you a hand.
But if you keep on hurting me,
You can never be my friend.

by Itka Frajman Zygmuntowicz February 24, 1978
Copyright 1996

I Can't Be You

I can't be you
And you can't be me.
For each human being is different
Just like each tree.

God does not create
Copies or reproductions.
Originality and uniqueness
Are the world's attractions.

Among so many millions
Of people you see,
There is only one special you
And only one special me.

by Itka Frajman Zygmuntowicz   June 30, 1994
Copyright 1996

Do Not Forget Us

A number is tattooed for life on my arm,
On my mind, my heart, my soul.
I remember the killing center of Auschwitz
And the six million voices that call.

Do not forget us!

Do not forget us!

The voices are pleading,
Voices of our beloved families, relatives and friends,
So savagely transformed to numbers and to ashes
By the bloody Nazi hands.

Do not forget us!

The voices pursue me,
I hear them so loud and clear.
Can the horrors of the Holocaust be forgotten?
No! Not as long as we are still here!

Do not forget us!

Dear sisters and brothers,
To carry our message on
Even when we the last of the last
To our eternal rest will have gone.

Do not forget us! Please.

by Itka Frajman Zygmuntowicz   May 27, 1978
Copyright 1996

I Am Not a Number

I was trapped in the killing center of Auschwitz,
Surrounded by barbed wires, gas chambers, smoke and flame;
The Nazis tattooed a number on my arm,
25673 became my new name.

They tried to reduce me to a number,
Dehumanize me day by day;
But regardless of all their efforts,
They could not take my self-worth away.

They murdered in the gas chamber my entire family,
In one single day;
All my earthly possessions,
Were so brutally taken away.

They treated me worse than a hardened criminal
Even though I did not commit any crime;
They hated me merely for being born Jewish
And starved and tortured me all the time.

I was only thirteen years old
When they took away from me my right to life;
But they could not take away my will
To live and to survive.

For nearly six nightmarish years
I endured a living hell;
Nevertheless, I've outlived Hitler and the Third Reich
And lived my story to tell.

by Itka Frajman Zygmuntowicz   May 27, 1978
Copyright 1996

For Everything There Is a Season

There is a time for joy
And a time for sorrow,
But there is never a time
To put off living until tomorrow.

There is a time for peace
And a time for war,
But the time that we wasted
We can never restore.

by Itka Frajman Zygmuntowicz   May 13, 1994
Copyright 1996

The Most Valuable Gift

Life is the most valuable gift of all.
We cannot buy it.
We cannot sell it.
We cannot exchange it.
We cannot postpone it.
But most importantly,
We can never, never replace it.

by Itka Frajman Zygmuntowicz   June 12, 1983
Copyright 1996

One Day I Shall Die

One day I shall die
And be no longer here,
My death will only matter
To those who held me dear.

How much they will miss me
Or remember me by
Will depend on the way I live
And on the way I'll die.

And on the little deeds
Of kindness and of help
And if I cared for others
Or only for myself.

I cannot stop death
For that is not in my power,
But I can make the most
Of every minute and hour.

by Itka Frajman Zygmuntowicz   December 15, 1966
Copyright 1996

Who Wrote On Your Arm?

"Who wrote on your arm, Mom?"
Asked curiously my little boy one day.
I looked sadly at my innocent child
And thought very carefully what to say.

"The Nazis tattooed this number on my arm,"
I told my son short and plain.
"Why did they do it, Mom?" he asked further,
"My God," I thought, "How can I explain?"

"You see, my child, there was a man,
Adolph Hitler was his name.
He was very cruel and hateful
And inflicted on people suffering and pain."

"Oh," said he and ran out to play
And I sighed with great relief.
I wanted to protect him for as long as I could
From knowing my deep sorrow and grief.

He grew and I could not protect him forever,
So I answered his questions one at a time.
He wanted to know why we Jews are hated;
Did we commit some kind of crime?

"No, my child," I told my son,
"We have not committed any crime.

Yet we Jews have been victimized and slaughtered
By Pharaohs, Hamans, and Hitlers all the time."

"Do you hate the Nazis for what they did to us?
Now I have no grandparents and relatives like my friends.
The Nazis murdered all our loved ones,
They have blood on their hands."

"I know, my child, that you too are hurting.
But hatred and revenge can never restore,
The lives of those who perished in the Holocaust
And the precious things we had before."

"You and I who know what pain is
Must never inflict on others hurt and pain.
We must try to build a better world
So the death of our six million shall not be in vain."

by Itka Frajman Zygmuntowicz   May 14, 1979
Copyright 1996

Puzzles

We are parts of a vast puzzle
Tossed into the world with others,
Though each of us is unique
We are all sisters and brothers.

Each of us is struggling to find
Our own special place,
To be ourselves, but to fit in with others
Is a challenge for the human race.

by Itka Frajman Zygmuntowicz   February 8, 1966
Copyright 1996

I Don't Want To Be Like Cain or Abel

I don't want to be killed like
 My brother Abel,

I don't want to be a killer like
 My brother Cain,

I want to be my brother's keeper
 And not to cause anyone suffering or pain,

I want to make this world
 A better place to live,

So that not one of God's children
 Should ever know my deep sorrow and grief.

by Itka Frajman Zygmuntowicz   May 13, 1983
Copyright 1996

I Know

From my Jewish roots
I've sucked my spiritual nourishment,
From my family who loved me unconditionally
I've learned how to love.

From the Nazis who hated me
Merely for being born Jewish
And murdered in Auschwitz my entire family,
I've learned how destructive hatred is.

I know how it feels to be starved and tortured,
I know how it feels to be homeless, and all alone,
I know what suffering is,
I know, I know!

by Itka Frajman Zygmuntowicz   May 20, 1978
Copyright 1996

Little Things

Little things mean so much
After they are gone.
Little things mean so much,
When you are all alone.

A little smile, a friendly call,
Or a birthday card,
Are little things
But they warm the heart.

Little things, precious things,
I miss you so today.
Since my loved ones are gone,
I long for yesterday.

Little things I took for granted
And now when they are gone.
Little things mean so much
When you are left alone.

by Itka Frajman Zygmuntowicz   Copyright 1996

Words and Deeds

Every human word and deed
Gets inscribed in the eternity of time,
And long after we are gone
All our words and deeds
Still affect the lives of those
Whom we have touched
And link themselves together
To the long human chain of eternity.

by Itka Frajman Zygmuntowicz   Copyright 1996

The Power of Words

Words are expressions of the heart and mind,
Powerful tools used by humankind
To teach, to inspire, to correct, and to inform,
To brainwash and to control, to negate and to affirm.

Words reveal and words conceal
The way we really think and feel.
Words entice, enchant and charm,
And words like bullets can kill and harm.

Words are tools to write poetry and prose,
Means to describe a lovely summer rose.
Words can hypnotize and cast a magic spell
And words can terrorize and create a living hell.

Words are connected with God, history, time, and places,
And are used by people of all races.
Words can inflict both pain and pleasure
And affect our lives beyond measure.

by Itka Frajman Zygmuntowicz June 14, 1987
Copyright 1996

The Secret of Finding Peace of Mind

We live in a world of life and death.
Every single second of every single day
And of every single night,
Someplace in the universe,
Someone gets born and someone dies,
Someone is happy and someone cries.
Life and death, pleasure and pain,
Joy and grief, love and hate,
Creation and destruction are all part of
the human condition.
To be human is to have limitations,
And to have the ability to accept our
limitations,
Is the secret of finding peace of mind.

by Itka Frajman Zygmuntowicz   January 29, 2000
Copyright 2000

Made in the USA
San Bernardino, CA
06 March 2014